Collection Editors:

Laure Mistral
Philippe Godard

Also Available:

We Live in China
We Live in India
We Live in Brazil

日本

We Live in
Japan

By Alexandre Messager

Illustrations by Sophie Duffet

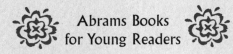

Abrams Books
for Young Readers

Presenting...Japan!

Japan is a country comprised of over 6,800 islands that stretch 3,800 kilometres across the sea. These islands are actually the summits of a long chain of underwater volcanic mountains that rise above the surface of the ocean. Because of this, 70 per cent of the land is mountainous. The highest peak is the volcano Mount Fuji (*Fuji-yama* or *Fuji-san*), which reaches an altitude of 3,776 metres. Ninety-six per cent of the Japanese population lives on one of the four main islands: Honshu, Shikoku, Kyūshū and Hokkaido.

Surface Area: Japan covers an area of 377,835 square kilometres (99 per cent land, 1 per cent water), which is about 1.5 times the size of the United Kingdom.

Population: In 2005, Japan's population was estimated to be 127.5 million – over twice as many people as in the UK. The population density is one of the highest in the world, with 329.5 people per square kilometre, or 1.35 times higher than in the UK. Interestingly, Japan has the longest life expectancy in the world. On average, women live to be 85 and men live to be 78.

Official Language: Japanese.

Major Religions: Approximately 85 per cent of Japanese practise both Shinto and Buddhism, although Buddhism can be seen both as a philosophy and a religion. Less than 1 per cent of the population practise Christianity.

Major Cities: Japan is an urban society. Some cities are so large that they touch; these are called 'conurbations'. For example, Tokyo, the most populated city in the world, has merged into Yokohama; 33.4 million people live in the Tokyo-Yokohama conurbation.

Climate: Like Britain, Japan has a temperate climate, with four distinct seasons.

Earthquakes, Tsunamis and Typhoons: There are often earthquakes in Japan. Depending upon their intensity, earthquakes can cause tidal waves, which are called tsunamis. Each September near the end of the month, there is also a period of strong winds, which are called typhoons. These storms often cause enormous amounts of damage.

Legendary Beginnings

Japan, or the 'Land of the Rising Sun', is an archipelago comprised of thousands of islands that, according to legend, was created by the goddess Izanami. One day, she plunged her spear into the ocean. When she pulled it out, the drops of water that fell from the spear became islands, forming the archipelago of Japan.

No-one knows the exact origins of the Japanese people. The first inhabitants of the archipelago were the Ainu, the people who now live in the north of the country, on the island of Hokkaido.

For most of its history, Japan has been an isolated country. For a long time, China and Korea were its only links with the outside world. This isolation was a result of its geographical situation.

Japan established trade links with China very early on, in 57 BCE – Chinese culture has thus greatly influenced Japanese culture. It was only in 1549 that the first Western ships, belonging to Portuguese traders, sailed into Japanese ports. At this point in history, the Portuguese were the world's greatest sailors. They had already made contact with a number of Asian countries, in particular Indonesia, in order to buy spices. But Japan's emperor reacted immediately to the intrusion of Portuguese ships in Japanese waters. He closed all ports and forbade the Japanese to leave their islands, in order to prevent the strangers from exerting even the slightest influence on the country. Then, in 1639, under pressure from the Japanese lords (the shoguns) who were afraid of losing their power, Japan was closed entirely to foreigners.

It was only in 1853, following the sudden emergence of the United States Navy on its coast, that Japan reopened to the world. The Meiji Emperor, who wanted to modernise Japanese society and feared that his country was lagging behind the rest of the world, decided that it was time to take stock of what exactly the West could offer Japan. Japanese were thus sent to Europe and America to learn more about the best aspects of Western civilisation. After just several years, Japanese society was completely transformed. In 1905, their victory over Russia in the Russo-Japanese War proved that Japan had become a world power.

At the beginning of the Second World War, Japan was initially neutral. However, Germany's success encouraged them to be more aggressive. Beginning with a surprise attack on Pearl Harbor, the US naval base in the Pacific Ocean, Japan proceeded to invade a number of Asian countries. It was only in 1945, after two nuclear bombs were dropped on Hiroshima and Nagasaki, that Japan finally surrendered. Since then, Japan has never again had an army. However, in 2004, a contingent of the Japan Self-Defense Forces was sent to Iraq to help US troops.

Japan changed completely following the Second World War. The Japanese rebuilt their war-torn country and developed big industries: cars, boats, trains, televisions, computers, video games and electronics. Today, it has become an industrial power that exerts an economic and cultural supremacy over a large part of the world. Japan is the country with the world's fastest trains (the *Shinkansen*) and is where the Internet is the most developed. Nevertheless, this ultramodern country has kept a number of its old traditions very much alive.

Aoki, Hayo and Kenji
Invite Us to Visit Japan

These three children live on Honshu, the main island of the archipelago.

Aoki lives in Tokyo, the capital of Japan, in a building located in the Minato-ku ward, right in the heart of downtown. Once a year, she goes on holiday to visit her aunt in Sapporo, a city on the island of Hokkaido in the north of Japan. Hokkaido is where the first inhabitants of the archipelago lived.

Hayo lives in Kyoto, the imperial city. He knows a lot about the history of his country. He especially loves the medieval period – the age of the samurai. His mother is a specialist in tea ceremonies and in *ikebana*, the art of flower arrangements. She teaches Ogino, Hayo's sister, so that she can continue these traditions. Hayo dreams of becoming a *sumotori*, a sumo wrestler.

Kenji lives in Hiroshima, in a small building near the port. The city of Hiroshima is known throughout the world, because it was where the first atomic bomb in history was dropped, on 6 August 1945. Every year at school, Kenji commemorates Sadako Sasaki, a young victim of this tragedy.

Aoki Lives in Tokyo

Aoki was born eleven years ago in Tokyo, the capital of Japan. She lives in a ten-storey building in the Minato-ku ward, in the heart of the city. There are many offices, hotels and businesses in this area.

Tokyo is a megalopolis, a 'mega-city'! It is the biggest city in the world, with more than 30 million residents. It would take Aoki years and years to explore every street and alleyway. Japan is only one and a half times larger than the United Kingdom, but it's much more populated, with 128 million inhabitants!

The Different Faces of Tokyo

Tokyo is divided into wards, each with its own characteristics.

Shinjuku is one of the most modern wards in Tokyo, with giant neon signs that blink night and day, and enormous television screens on the sides of buildings. There are always throngs of people in the street, and even at night you have the impression that life here never lets up!

The tallest buildings in Tokyo are in Shinjuku, and the headquarters of the most important Japanese companies can be found here. Aoki's father works in an insurance company which has offices on the fifty-fifth floor of one of the buildings.

From up there you can admire the views over Tokyo Bay and look down on the many buildings. In Shinjuku you can also find department stores, restaurants, video arcades and nightclubs.

The Ueno district, in contrast, is much more traditional and much calmer, with very few office buildings – it is mostly houses and parks. Last spring, Aoki's class went on a picnic to Ueno Park, which is famous for its blossoming cherry trees. Sometimes you can find futuristic buildings next to a Buddhist pagoda or a cluster of traditional Japanese wooden houses, all in the same district. It's a little like a big village that's tucked away in the middle of an extremely modern city. But Tokyo's strangest feature is in the Aoyama district, close to where Aoki lives: the *Tokyo Tower*. It's a replica of the Eiffel Tower in Paris, and was built in 1958 as a broadcasting antenna for television and radio.

Right next to Tokyo is the city of Yokohama, the largest port in Japan. The two cities are so close that you can't tell where one ends and the other begins. Aoki and her parents often go for a walk in Yokohama at the weekend to admire Tokyo Bay and watch the gigantic freighters coming into port. Once or twice per year, Aoki's family gets up very early, at about five o'clock, to go to the all-night fish market there.

Earthquakes

There are often earthquakes in Japan. One popular legend tells of a giant catfish, *Namazu*, who lives under the ground and causes earthquakes whenever he moves his tail.

In 1923, Tokyo was devastated by an earthquake that claimed over 100,000 victims. In 1995, the city of Kōbe was also hit by a quake, causing many deaths. Thankfully, major earthquakes like these are rare, and most are not dangerous at all. What's more, the Japanese construct buildings with special reinforcements designed to help them endure most tremors. This is effective even when the buildings are very tall.

Sometimes, Aoki and her family are awoken in the middle of the night because the walls and doors are vibrating, and the beds are shaking. Most of the time, this only lasts a few seconds, but sometimes it can be really frightening. If the tremors are strong, you have to open a window quickly so that you are able to leave in case the front door gets stuck afterwards. Then you should take shelter under a table so you don't get hurt by any falling objects. You should never go outside until the earthquake is over.

Each morning, Aoki walks to school, because she's lucky enough to live close by, which isn't the case for many children.

Aoki eats breakfast with her parents, but without her big brother, Shinji. He always wakes up late and often has to run to make sure he gets to school on time!
Like all Japanese children, Aoki has been going to school since the age of five. She's in the last year of primary school, which lasts six years. Then, she will go to middle school where she will begin to learn English. Three years later, she will go to high school.

Unlike the United Kingdom, the school year begins in April and ends in March. There are not a lot of holidays, only one month in summer. Aoki goes to an all-girls school. But in her brother's high school, there are both boys and girls. In Japanese schools, the children all wear uniforms. Boys wear trousers and a jacket, while the girls wear skirts with a blazer. The uniforms help promote equality among the children.

In Aoki's school, like in all Japanese schools, the rules are very strict. Even when she was very young, Aoki learned to greet her teachers (*sensei*) by bowing before them as a sign of respect. Teachers represent knowledge and wisdom, and it is the custom to always obey them. This is also a way to pay homage to their age: the elders must be respected. Teachers, for their part, are very attentive towards children.

What Aoki likes most at school are the group callisthenics every morning, and classes in *origami* (the art of paper folding) where she learns to fold paper squares into animals, dolls and boats, without using scissors or glue. This is an exercise in precision and skill that demands quite a bit of concentration.

Example of *origami*.

Evening Classes

Beginning in middle school, competition between students becomes fierce, because they all want to go to the best schools and universities in the country.

At the end of each academic year, the children take exams; the results of the exams are then evaluated and used to determine which school the students will go to. They are thus constantly under pressure. In Japanese schools, there is an expression that everyone uses: *juken jigoku*, or 'examination hell'. In Japanese culture, success is something of extreme importance and failure is often still perceived to be a matter of shame or, even worse, dishonour.

When Aoki comes back home from school in the evening, she only sees her brother Shinji for a couple of minutes. This is because, like many students, he goes to a private cram school, where he prepares for his exams. These evening classes, called *juku*, are attended by many students who want to prepare for the entrance examinations for the best schools and universities in Tokyo. Next year when Aoki starts middle school, it will be her turn to go to evening classes.

Before going to see his teacher, Shinji wolfs down a *bento*, a 'boxed lunch' that his mother has made for him. The *bento*, usually served in a

small red box, is very popular in Japan. At any time of day, but particularly at lunch, the Japanese can be seen eating their *bento*. The ubiquitous, tiny red boxes contain different dishes depending on the region that you are in. In general, a *bento* includes pieces of chicken or raw fish, and an assortment of cooked and pickled vegetables. Shinji's mother often prepares him a sweet omelette and fish with rice. Shinji eats his dinner very early, because by the time his evening classes are over it is late, and all he wants is to return home and go to bed.

Japanese Writing

At school, Aoki learns how to read and write *kanji*, the characters used in the Japanese written language.

Spread by Buddhist monks who came to Japan beginning in the fourth century, *kanji* are complex ideograms, the same as those used in written Chinese. Many of the early characters were originally images or pictures. For example, the word 'volcano' is represented by the *kanji* meaning 'fire' placed next to the *kanji* meaning 'mountain': put a fire next to a

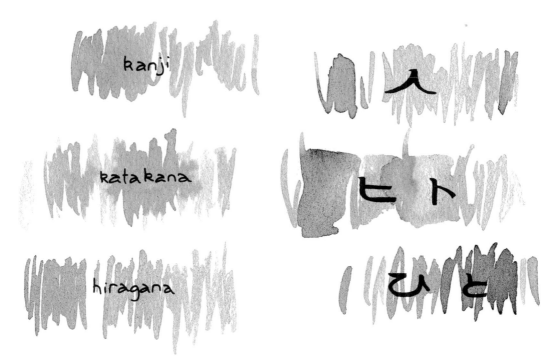

The word 'man' written in *kanji, katakana* and *hiragana*.

mountain and you've got a volcano! Aoki already knows five hundred *kanji,* and by the time she finishes high school, she will know at least two thousand.

But the Japanese writing system is not only made up of *kanji.* After having temporarily cut off their relations with China around 838, the Japanese invented other symbols that were simpler and better adapted to their way of life. When you look at Japanese writing today, in addition to *kanji,* you will see other, less-complex characters, *katakana* and *hiragana.* So in order to write Japanese, you have to use the straight-lined ideograms, *kanji,* as well as the simpler and more cursive *katakana* and *hiragana.*

At school, Aoki first learned *hiragana,* which are simpler. It was by using these characters that she learned to read and write Japanese. Then her teacher taught her the *kanji* that are easiest to write and remember. When she goes to middle school, she will learn *katakana* in addition to other *kanji.* For now, though, Aoki reads stories written only with *hiragana* and *kanji* – specifically *manga,* Japanese comic books.

Manga

Like all children her age, Aoki loves to read *manga*, which are easy to understand because of the illustrations and writing that only uses *hiragana*.

But *manga* aren't just for children: there are also *manga* for teenagers and even for adults. Aoki's brother and parents read them too. In Japan, everyone reads *manga* – at home, in the subway, in parks and even in the street. It's a real cultural phenomenon; there are comic books written about everything!

***Manga* have been popular in Japan for a very long time.** It first started in 710, when *manga* were rolls of paper (*emakimono*), on which illustrations were drawn together with text. As you unrolled the paper, a story would appear. In the beginning, *manga* were shown in the emperor's court, before eventually becoming more common. But it was only at the start of the twentieth century that *manga* appeared in their current form, which is like a comic book. Before the Second World War, the most famous *manga* were *Norakuro* (The Black Dog) and *Boken Dankichi* (The Adventures of Dankichi). Aoki's grandfather loved these comics, and he gave them to his granddaughter as soon as she could read.

After the Second World War, *manga* became much more animated, with characters constantly in motion, very short sentences and onomatopoeia (words that imitate the sounds they are associated with, like 'Pow!'). In 1963, *Tetsuwan Atomu* (Astro Boy) became the first televised *manga*, just like *Peanuts* became a cartoon after first starting out as a comic strip. Today, there are many *manga* characters on television and in video games.

The Ainu: The First Inhabitants of Japan

Once a year, during the summer holidays, Aoki goes to visit her Aunt Kusama, who lives on the island of Hokkaido in Sapporo.

This island is in the far north of Japan, and is close to Russia. Because of snow storms it gets very cold in winter, but in summer, it is warm and dry. Many Japanese tourists like to come here on holiday because of the climate.

Each year, this trip is an opportunity for Aoki and her mother to fly in a plane, passing over the many mountains and volcanoes near Sapporo. Kusama, Aoki's aunt, was born in Hokkaido and is the descendant of an Ainu village chief.

Aoki visits the village of Asahikawa close to Sapporo. It is a reconstructed Ainu village that shows their traditional way of life. Aunt Kusama, who knows the history of the Ainu well, tells how they are considered to be the indigenous inhabitants of the Japanese islands. They came from Siberia, and they have lighter skin than Japanese people. Several thousand years ago, they settled in Hokkaido, as well as the neighbouring Kuril Islands and the island of Sakhalin, which today belong to Russia.

The Ainu have always tried to maintain their independence. They were mainly hunters and fishermen. On Hokkaido and in the northern part of Honshu, they built thousands of small villages. But the Ainu were not alone for very long: people from Asia, specifically China and Korea, also began settling on the Japanese archipelago, and little by little they began moving onto the Ainu's land.

In the fifth century, the Ainu were persecuted by the imperial court; in the ninth century they were persecuted again by the Fujiwara family. The Fujiwaras were powerful shogun, or military lords. At this point in history they controlled Japan, and they also tried to take control of the Ainu land in the far north. In the nineteenth century, the Japanese government was still trying to expand its territory: this time, they decided to colonise Ainu land and to end their independence once and for all. Major forests were turned into farm land, and deprived of their hunting grounds, many of the Ainu could no longer survive. Those that lived had no choice but to learn how to farm.

Today, there are only several thousand Ainu left. They are trying to preserve what remains of their cultural heritage. Aunt Kusama, who is Ainu, fought for many years so that the Japanese government would recognise the rights and identity of her people. In 1997, Japan accepted to promote Ainu culture. But this is not enough, and today Aoki's aunt continues to give lectures in Tokyo or Kyoto, to talk about her ancestors so that their history is not forgotten.

Following Aunt Kusama's advice, Aoki has decided to give a presentation on the Ainu when she goes back to school after the holidays.

Hayo Lives in Kyoto, the Imperial City

Kyoto was the capital of Japan for a very long time, from 794 to 1868. In fact, in Japanese, Kyoto means 'capital city'. Hayo, an eleven-year-old boy, and his sister, Ogino, who is thirteen, live in Kyoto. Their parents run a *ryokan*: a traditional inn close to Gion, the historic district.

Like all *ryokan*, the one that belongs to Hayo's family is a large, traditional house that is two storeys tall and built entirely of wood. There are fourteen guestrooms, each named after a flower, like cherry blossom, jasmine and iris. Next to each guestroom there is also a small sitting room, where guests can drink tea and eat while seated on cushions. But what is really special about a *ryokan* is that you sleep on a *futon*, a traditional Japanese mattress that is put directly onto the floor, and then is folded up and put away after you get out of bed. There are two types of beds in Japan: *futon* and mattresses like the ones you have at home.

In Kyoto, the *ryokan* where Hayo and Ogino live is well known because it is one of the oldest; it has been passed down from generation to generation.

Much smaller than Tokyo, Kyoto is located close to two other large cities, Kōbe and Osaka. Together they make up the second largest conurbation in Japan. Today, Kyoto is well known because of an important conference that took place here in 1997, during which the 'Kyoto Protocol' was drawn up, an international treaty to fight global warming and pollution throughout the world.

The city is divided into three major sections: the business district in the south, the old town in the centre (where Hayo and Ogino live) and the parks in the north. Even with modernisation and the fact that it is no longer the capital of the country, Kyoto remains first and foremost the historic and cultural heart of Japan. The imperial city's historic monuments were designated UNESCO World Heritage Sites in 1994. Hayo and Ogino are proud to live in such a historic city.

Kyoto: A Monumental City

Hayo and Ogino have already visited many of the city's temples and palaces with their parents and grandparents. But there are just as many waiting to be discovered, because there are over two thousand temples and shrines in all!

Hayo and Ogino are already familiar with the most famous legacies of the imperial past: the emperor's palace; the shogun's palace, which looks like a fortified castle; the Golden Pavilion, whose roof and walls are covered in gold leaf; the Buddhist temple Ryoan-ji, renowned for its Zen garden of raked sand and rocks, which recalls islands adrift in a sea of waves; and the Silver Pavilion, with a Chinese-style landscape garden. During the feudal period, when Japanese society was quite hierarchical, all of the most prestigious places were reserved for the emperor, the court, the nobility and the Buddhist monks, who held great power.

Everyday in their parents' small hotel, Hayo and Ogino meet new foreign and Japanese tourists who have come to visit the imperial city. Sometimes, their father takes their guests to visit the most famous monuments. He tells them the history of the samurai, who lived in the period when the nobility shared Japan.

The Shogun and the Samurai

Ever since he was little, Hayo has listened to his father tell the story of the samurai, the most powerful and respected of warriors.

The word 'samurai' means 'he who serves'. These warriors influenced Japanese history from the twelfth century all the way up to the end of the nineteenth century. The time of the samurai began when Japan was divided into 'shogunates', territories controlled by the lords, or shogun. The shogun were military generals, and they defended their territory with the help of the samurai, formidable warriors who were loyal to their masters until death. But the samurai also served the emperor.

During this long period, there were many battles between shogunates. Some families tried to extend their power, and the samurai fought incessantly. Those who belonged to the richest and most powerful shogunates fought on horseback, the others were on foot. The samurai wore helmets designed to frighten their enemies, and their flexible armour was made of thin steel plates that were laced or riveted together. Only the samurai were allowed to use the supreme weapons of war, two swords worn on the left side: the *daito* (the long sword), which was used to fight, and the *shoto* (the short sword), which was used to cut off the head of a defeated samurai.

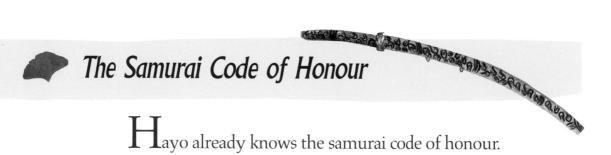

The Samurai Code of Honour

Hayo already knows the samurai code of honour.

His father explained to him that under the rule of the shogunates, Japanese society was very hierarchical. Apart from the emperor, who was descended from the gods, the most powerful men were the nobility governing the shogunates. The shogun themselves were placed in a hierarchy according to the amount of territory and money they owned; then came the craftsmen, the farmers and the merchants; at the bottom of the ladder were the eta, those who did the work that no-one else would do.

Samurai held a place of privilege. They didn't have the right to work or earn money; they were required to devote themselves to noble tasks, which was essentially to fight for their lord. Highly organised, they had a code of conduct and strict rules. A samurai could never hesitate to cut off the head of someone who had acted wrongly towards him, and he needed to be ready to lend his muscle, intelligence and assets to both the emperor and his master. 'To live and die with the sword in hand', was the samurai motto. The greatest dishonour for a samurai was to be taken prisoner. If this happened, he would prefer to commit suicide.

The Art of Flower Arrangement

In the inn run by Hayo's parents, each room is decorated with a bouquet of flowers or plants. Some are very simple, others very sophisticated.

In Japan, the art of flower arrangement (*ikebana*, which literally means 'living flowers') is an old tradition that is still popular. Like many Japanese traditions, *ikebana* was imported from China by Buddhist monks in the seventh century. At this time, floral art was reserved for men. The times have changed though, because today it is practised especially by young girls and women.

Hayo's mother gives classes in flower arrangement at the oldest
ikebana school in Japan, the Ikenobo School in Kyoto. With the help
of her mother, Hayo's sister, Ogino, spends her time at home trying
to arrange flower bouquets. Using the branches, leaves and flowers,
the object is to create a bouquet that symbolises heaven, earth and
humankind, not an easy feat.

Ogino knows that when the stems are under water, the flowers stay
fresh longer. She also lightly burns or steams the stems to make them
stiffer so that the bouquets last longer.

Towards the end of the year, Hayo and Ogino watch their mother
prepare dozens of bouquets that are displayed at the entrance to the
hotel. She mostly uses chrysanthemums and pine branches, because
one of the rules of *ikebana* is to use the plants that best represent the
actual season. For the Doll Festival (or Girls' Day) in March, Ogino
prepares a bouquet with peach or cherry branches. The colour and the
shape of the vase are also very important, because the vase must match
the flowers that are used.

In July, in the Gion district (close to where Hayo's family lives), you can see the most beautiful flower arrangements in Kyoto. It is the biggest festival in the city, and for two days there are parades, floats and musicians. Many lanterns and floral banners are hung in front of house windows. It is an old festival that dates back to 869, and it is very famous in Japan. It originally served to bring the city's inhabitants together to fight a plague ravaging Kyoto and the surrounding towns. It is a festival that celebrates life.

Thankfully, the plague has not returned. Even today, the Gion Festival brings the people of Kyoto together to celebrate life with flowers.

 ## The Tea Ceremony

Hayo and Ogino's hotel is not only known for its bouquets: their mother is also a specialist in *chanoyu*, the tea ceremony.

Tea was imported from China by Buddhist monks in the eighth century and the tea ceremony began to take root in Japan from the twelfth century onwards. Since then, for the majority of Japanese, *chanoyu* is the tradition that best reflects Japanese values: refinement, harmony with nature, aesthetics, art, respect for others, meditation and philosophy. Considered as one way to attain *wabi*, a state in which you find peace and tranquillity through simplicity, the tea ceremony is a true art.

For Hayo and Ogino, the *chanoyu* is an important moment, during which they have the feeling that they are part of a beautiful tradition. They take turns helping their mother to welcome guests and to prepare tea.

In accordance with tradition, a small pavilion dedicated to the tea ceremony was specially built in the shady part of the hotel garden. The ritual is the same for each ceremony. The guests spend several minutes observing nature in the garden. Then, at the entrance to the pavilion, they take off their shoes. The doorway is particularly small, not higher than sixty centimetres – this encourages guests to bow before entering. This is a natural way for them to shed their pride and to encourage humility. Once inside, they move forward in a kneeling position.

Once all the guests are seated in the formal kneeling position, known as *seiza*, Ogino or Hayo offers small sweet cakes. Then their mother pours hot water into a teapot containing powdered green tea, or *matcha*. Each guest tastes the tea in a ceramic bowl, the *chawan*, and then slightly turns it clockwise three times with the right hand, so that they can admire the different sides of the bowl. When the bowl is empty, each guest turns it in the opposite direction before giving it back to Hayo's mother. She then shows the guests the utensils used to prepare the tea: the spatula, whisk and the teapot. This ritual, which is extremely precise, generally takes place in silence in order to encourage meditation.

The tea ceremony, which lasts from thirty to forty minutes, must be a harmonious moment. Many Japanese hold them at home; sometimes they have several in one day, with different members of their family or friends that have dropped by to visit. Guests are welcomed in a room designed just for this, which is called a *chanoma*.

Like many *ryokan* hosts, Hayo and Ogino's mother must hold several ceremonies in a row. When the small pavilion is empty, Ogino practices greeting her brother. She also wants to become a specialist in the tea ceremony, and, in order to do this, she must perfect each gesture.

 ## Hayo Dreams of Becoming a Sumotori

Hayo loves his country's traditions, and the one that he likes the best is sumo.

In Japan, sumo is a national sport; it is as popular as football in the United Kingdom, or baseball in the United States. Every year, six major tournaments are held in Tokyo, Osaka, Nagoya and Fukuoka.

Hayo and his father go to the one in Osaka, the closest city to Kyoto. Each tournament is a huge event watched by millions of Japanese. One of Hayo's favourite moments is the opening pre-fight ceremony, when the *sumotori* (wrestlers) form a circle around the wrestling ring and are presented to the public. Hayo has all the time to watch them... and dream that one day he will become a *Yokozuna*, the highest rank in sumo.

According to legend, sumo was born 2,500 years ago when two gods fought one another for possession of the islands in the Japanese archipelago. At first, sumo matches took place in the villages in order to obtain the blessings of the gods for the coming harvests. Then tournaments were held at more and more places, during which wrestlers from all over Japan would pit their strength against each other. It became an official sport in the Heian period (794-1185).

The two sumo wrestlers fight in an area marked by a circle, a kind of ring. Before the fight begins, the *sumotori* face each other and throw salt on to the ring to cleanse all impurities, before drinking water from a ladle. Then, each combatant raises a leg to stomp on the ground, a symbolic way of crushing any evil spirits that might be nearby. The fight begins at the signal of the referee, who is in the centre of the ring.

After a period of observation, the wrestlers touch the ground with their hands to accept the combat. Then the fight can begin, and the two *sumotori* charge towards each other. The goal of each wrestler is to either throw his opponent out of the ring or knock him down to the ground. Contrary to its appearance, sumo is a very technical sport.

Sumo, which is based on very specific rules and rituals is also a very difficult way of life. Hayo already knows that if he wants to become a *sumotori*, he must go to a sumo school after high school. For several years he will live in a kind of commune and train every day with his companions. As a young wrestler, he must also cook, clean and follow his elders' orders. Finally, he has to gain a lot of weight, because sumo wrestlers must be very strong. In order to do this, he has to eat the same dish several times a day, called a *chankonabe*. This is a recipe that is kept secret by the sumo masters, and it includes vegetables, meat and fish. Hayo must also let his hair grow, because sumo wrestlers have to have long hair, slicked back with oil and tied up in a topknot. Finally, from morning to night and during tournaments, he can only wear a *mawashi*, a piece of fabric wrapped around the waist and between the legs.

Hayo still has time before becoming a sumo wrestler. In any case, he must finish high school before he can begin sumo school. In the meantime, he occasionally tries out his wrestling skills with his best friend, Yukio.

Kenji Lives in Hiroshima, The City of Peace

Kenji is twelve years old. He lives in a flat with his parents, close to the port of Hiroshima, which is one of the most important in Japan. From the balcony in his room, Kenji can see the enormous bay dotted with small islands.

Even with all the industry that has developed along the bay, there are still lots of small oyster farms. Kenji's grandfather owns several oyster farms and sells his harvest to the restaurants in town. Kenji's father is a taxi driver and his mother is a secretary in a small clothing company. Kenji's ancestors have always lived in Hiroshima, ever since it was founded several centuries ago.

Hiroshima will always be remembered for the tragedy of 6 August 1945. On that day, it was destroyed by the first atomic bomb in history. Several days later, a second bomb exploded in Nagasaki. This terrible tragedy also marked the end of the second World War; Japan surrendered immediately. Years later, the Japanese baptised Hiroshima the 'City of Peace', with the prayer that the nuclear bomb will never again be used in the world.

6 August 1945

The city of Hiroshima, founded by a powerful shogun in the sixteenth century, was a fortified city.

Later, it became an important urban centre during the Meiji period, in the second half of the nineteenth century. In the First and Second World Wars it was one of the main Japanese military bases. This is why it was the target of American air strikes.

On 6 August 1945, the American bomber *Enola Gay* dropped the first nuclear bomb in history, *Little Boy*. The explosion flattened the city instantly. More than 70,000 buildings and houses were destroyed, and 75,000 people were killed. In the weeks, months and years that followed, thousands of other people died of the after effects. More than 250,000 residents of Hiroshima died as a result of the atom bomb. Three days later, on 9 August 1945, a second nuclear bomb was dropped on the city of Nagasaki, where thousands of people died.

Kenji's grandfather was seven years old when the atom bomb was dropped on Hiroshima. He is a *hibakusha*, a bomb survivor. He was very lucky that day: he was exposed to very little radiation because his parents lived on the outskirts of Hiroshima

Today, he often goes for walks in Peace Memorial Park, which was inaugurated close to the spot where the bomb exploded. Sometimes, he takes Kenji with him to see the Flame of Peace that burns day and night, and which will stay lit as long as nuclear weapons continue to exist in the world. One day, when the two of them were walking, Kenji asked him about 6 August 1945.

'Grandfather, what were you doing that day when it happened? Were you still asleep?'

'No, I was in our courtyard with my mother who was hanging laundry. I remember her saying that the sky was *strangely quiet. Suddenly, we saw an enormous flash of yellow light, as bright as ten thousand suns. Then a dust cloud rose above the city; it was horrifying, it looked like the end of the world.'*

'Were you scared?'

'Not at first, because no-one knew what had happened. Then we saw hundreds of people arriving who were completely deformed; their clothing was torn, and they walked as best as they could just to leave the city. They didn't know where to go. My mother took in many people because they no longer had anywhere to live, everything had been destroyed. You can't imagine what a horrible sight it was.'

Sadako Sasaki and a Thousand Cranes

In Peace Memorial Park, there is a monument dedicated to all the children who were victims of the terrible bomb.

It depicts a young girl, Sadako Sasaki, standing on a granite stone and holding a golden crane in her outstretched arms. This crane evokes both a legend and the story of a little girl from Hiroshima. Among the Hiroshima bomb victims, there were thousands of children, who either died during the explosion or afterwards, when they fell ill with leukaemia, a type of cancer caused by radiation. Sadako Sasaki is a symbol thereof. She is not only remembered in Peace Memorial Park, but also in schools, like the one Kenji goes to, where small plaques engraved with Sadako's name hang in the corridors. Like all Japanese children, Kenji knows her story by heart.

Born in January 1943, Sadako was only two and a half when the atom bomb exploded in Hiroshima. On that day, she was in her room, just two kilometres from the explosion. Most of her neighbours were killed, but neither Sadako nor her parents were harmed. Years passed and the little girl grew up normally. She was a very good athlete and an especially fast runner, and she began to participate in competitions.
But one day in 1955 – when she was just twelve – she suddenly felt extremely tired and dizzy after completing a race. Her parents thought that the vertigo was just due to the exhaustion from running. But soon after she began having other dizzy spells, and one day she collapsed. Her parents took her to the hospital, where she was diagnosed with leukaemia, the 'atom bomb disease'.

Sadako's best friend, Chizuko, told her the ancient Japanese legend of one thousand cranes. In Japan, the crane is a very important and respected animal because it symbolises long life. It's said that if you fold one thousand origami cranes, the gods will be pleased and your wish will be granted. Sadako started folding paper cranes immediately, hoping that once she had folded one thousand paper cranes, the gods would cure her disease and let her start running again.

Sadako's family came to visit her in the hospital often, to talk with her and help fold the cranes. After she had folded five hundred, she felt better, and the doctors told her she could go home for a short while. But her dizzy spells began again, and she had to return to the hospital. Sadako spent several months folding a total of 644 paper cranes, before she died on 25 October 1955.

Sadako's story spread throughout Hiroshima, and her classmates finished folding the thousand cranes. Then they sold them, and with the money they earned they built a statue in honour of Sadako and all the children affected by the atom bomb. Today, the paper crane is the international symbol of peace. Following Sadako's death, children from across the world began folding cranes and sending them to Hiroshima. Every year in school, Kenji and his classmates spend one day folding dozens of cranes, before going to place them in Peace Memorial Park.

Shinto and Zen Buddhism

Like many Japanese, Kenji's family practise both Shinto and Buddhism.

Several months after he was born, Kenji's parents took him to a Shinto priest who blessed him in the name of several gods. Shinto, which means 'the way of the gods', is based on the belief in a number of gods, or spirits, connected to a particular place or natural element, like Amaterasu, the Goddess of the Sun. The gods represent the flow of energy that animates the universe and which gives life to nature, including plants, rocks and animals.

Kenji's parents put up a shrine (*kamidana*) in the entrance of their flat to worship the gods. In the middle of the shrine are a miniature Shinto temple and a number of good-luck charms: a small bamboo rake that helps you catch luck, a small red cow made out of papier-mâché to ward off evil, and even a small boat meant to bring treasure. There are also several small branches of *sakaki*, a sacred tree with the power to attract gods. Kenji often does a drawing that he places at the foot of the shrine so that the spirits stay for the longest possible time in their flat.

On New Year's Day, Kenji's family goes to a Shinto temple to pray for the New Year. In the hall designated for making offerings, Kenji places an arrow to which he has attached a piece of paper with a wish written on it. The Japanese say that this arrow has the power to banish evil spirits and grant your wish.

Kenji and his parents also practice Buddhism, which is above all considered to be a philosophy and a 'science of the spirit' rather than a religion. In Japan, Buddhism and Shinto became more and more entwined over the years. In the twelfth century, Zen Buddhism, an offshoot of traditional Buddhism, was brought back from China and began to develop following the creation of five monasteries in Japan. It took on the name *zazen*, which means 'to sit in meditation'. *Zazen* is a popular practice and there are thousands of temples throughout Japan. Sometimes, instead of going to a hotel or *ryokan*, some Western tourists spend the night in temples where they can learn *zazen*, under the guidance of a master.

Practicing Zazen

Kenji and his father go to a temple two nights a week to practice *zazen*. This is common in Japan, not only among Zen Buddhists, but also among those who seek some form of spiritual training.

Zazen is a philosophy and an art of meditation. In English, the word 'Zen' is sometimes used to mean detachment or serenity; it is a synonym for the word 'calm'.

When Kenji and his father enter the temple, they greet the people who are present by putting their palms together and bowing slightly, out of respect. Then they sit on the floor, with the monks and other Buddhists like them. Sometimes there are even foreign tourists. Kenji's father taught him how to sit and breathe correctly at home. At the temple, a teacher helps him master this. Knowing how to sit and breathe correctly are two things that are very important in *zazen*.

Kenji sits cross-legged in the 'lotus' position, with his right foot on his left thigh, and his left foot on his right thigh. His knees touch the ground and he must sit very straight, as if he were pushing on the ground with his knees and up towards the sky with his head. Then he closes his eyes slightly. His left hand rests on his right hand, the palms facing upwards. Each detail is important because all parts of the body are connected, and influence one another. The body must be totally stable in order to focus on meditation.

The most important part of *zazen* is breathing. There are several techniques. Kenji learned the simplest one, called *shoshuten*: he inhales deeply and follows his breath moving up his spine until it reaches the spot between his two eyes. He holds his breath and imagines a warm light, like the sun. Kenji then exhales slowly and starts over. It is not long before his breathing is calm, powerful and natural.

Sometimes, when Kenji is meditating, a 'master' or assistant strikes him lightly with the *jikido* (the sword of wisdom) on the right shoulder to indicate that he is sitting incorrectly. In silence, he adjusts his posture and begins meditating again, trying not to think about anything else. As his father says, *zazen* has no goal. It simply helps you to become more peaceful. After each session, Kenji has the feeling that his spirit is as clear as a cloudless sky.

The Game of Go
and the Spirit of Japanese Philosophy

Kenji wanted to learn to play *go* ever since reading a *manga* about Hikaru, a boy of his age.

One day, Hiraku finds an old *go* board, or *goban*, in his attic. He thinks it is particularly beautiful and decides to take it down to his room. Soon after, Hikaru learns that the board is possessed by a mysterious ghost named Sai, an ancient *go* master who taught the emperor in the Heian period, around 850. The ghost makes Hikaru play *go*, teaching him the best moves. Sometime later at a tournament, Hikaru faces the talented Akira and beats him. From this point on, a great rivalry develops between the two players; each one tries to learn the best strategies in order to become the best *go* master. Hikaru is helped by the ghost Sai, who has been searching for the 'divine move' for over one thousand years.

Fascinated by Hikaru's story, Kenji immediately wanted to learn to play *go* in a club.

According to legend, *go* was invented over four thousand years ago by two Chinese emperors, Yao and Shun, who wanted to impart wisdom to their sons at an early age. In fact, *go* is the oldest game in the world. At first, *go* was only played at the emperor's court, but later,

44

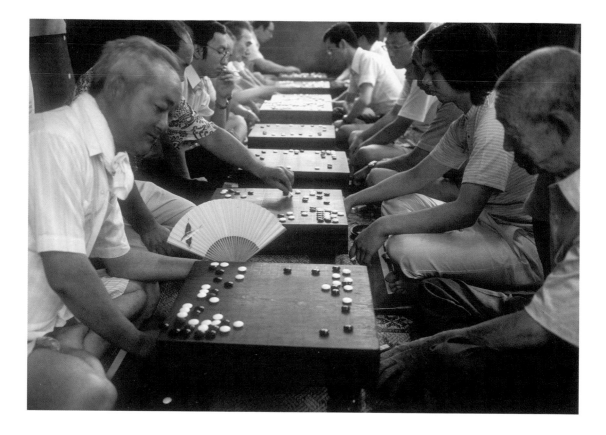

schools were founded throughout Japan. *Go* masters were very respected, and benefited from special privileges in the shoguns' courts. The Japanese like to say that *go* embodies the spirit of their philosophy perfectly. Actually, the game of *go* represents a way of life. It demands enormous mental discipline and long reflection, and is hugely popular. It is a complex, sophisticated game of strategy.

The first time that Kenji found himself in front of the neighbourhood club's *go* board, he was in awe. For one hour, an old master patiently explained to him the basic rules of the game. He told him that the two players must alternately place their black and white pieces on the board. In order to win, your pieces must control a larger territory than that of your opponent. But the bigger the territory, the harder it is to protect it from an opponent's attacks.

In *go*, there is no second place. At the end of the match, the winner is the one who, capable of blending attack and defence, has successfully expanded their own territory and reduced that of their opponent.

The loser is the one who recklessly sets out to conquer an area without having found a way to defend it.

After one hour of explanations and demonstrations, Kenji felt ready to play his first game. The old master, who has taught thousands of players in his life, explained to him that impatience is normal, because, after an hour of explanations, everyone thinks they know how to play *go*. But he told him that even one lifetime would not be enough to master the game. Kenji only understood this several minutes into the first game. Before he even had the time to realise what happened, the old master's black stones surrounded his white stones, which could no longer move.

When he came for his second class, Kenji knew that *go* is not a game of chance, and that luck does not matter. Like his hero, Hikaru, Kenji has begun to learn different strategies. Today, in spite of his young age, Kenji is already respected in the club. Like the ghost, Sai, his secret dream is to one day discover the 'divine move'.

Photographic credits:

p. 5 © Orion Press/Stone/Getty Images
p. 7 © Bob Rowan; Progressive Image/Corbis
p. 9 Rights reserved
p. 11 © Michael S. Yamashita/Corbis
p. 12 © Tom Wagner/Corbis
p. 19 © Akg-Images
p. 20/21 © Ed Freeman/Getty Images
p. 23 Rights reserved
p. 25 © Sam Clemens/Digital Vision/Getty Images
p. 30 © Hulton Archive/Getty Images
p. 32 © Kharbine-Tapabor/Coll. S. Kakou
p. 35 Rights reserved
p. 36 © Akg-Images
p. 38 © Akg-Images
p. 41 © Akg-Images/Suzanne Held
p. 46 © Hulton Archive/Getty Images

British Library Cataloguing-in-Publication Data
A catalogue record for this book is available from the British Library

ISBN: 0-8109-9344-9
ISBN13: 978-0-8109-9344-0

Copyright © 2006 Éditions de la Martinière, Paris
English translation copyright © 2006 Éditions de la Martinière, Paris
Typesetting for the English edition: Christophe Tardieux

Printed and bound in France by Pollina – n°L42145e
10 9 8 7 6 5 4 3 2 1

HNA ▰▰▰▰▰
harry n. abrams, inc.
a subsidiary of La Martinière Groupe